CU00867811

Disclaimer

This is a book by an educator intended for use by other educators. It is designed to be handed out to a class of 30+ middle school boys and girls (some of whom may not really want to be there) in a 45 minute-long introductory elective class. It does not contain a great deal of explanation or background on programming and is not really meant for individuals trying to learn on their own, though I believe it has value there, as well.

The design of this book allows teachers to engage the wide variety of students one finds in a middle school class. Most students will not take the time to read printed instructions (really, who does these days?), but can and will follow visual examples. This book makes use of that observation.

While I have used these tutorials day-in and day-out for three years (with, by my count, over 600 students), I don't simply hand them out and expect the students to do it on their own. I would suggest that the teacher study these tutorials beforehand and even make them along with the students on a display device.

Finally, these tutorials are meant as starting points – I generally require my students to make two or three changes to each program for full credit. Without doubt your students will discover new and interesting things to do with Scratch that you did not envision. Encourage and praise them when they do this. Such self-expression is (I think) what programming is really all about.

Dedications

First, to my Lord and Savior, Jesus Christ:
You are my reason for living. Any good I do comes from You.
"From You and through You and to You are all things.
To You be glory forever! Amen!" (Romans 11:36)

Second, to my wife of 14 years Tara: "Thanks" doesn't quite cover all that
you mean to me. I love being your husband!

Finally, to my kids, Kayleigh, Tyler, Zachary, Jarren, and Becca: Being your father
is one of the greatest blessings God has given to me! Remember life is good,
eternal life is better!

Table of Contents

What is Scratch?

Scratch is a computer programming language written by the Lifelong Kindergarten group at the MIT Media Lab. It was introduced in 2007 with the goal of introducing students to programming languages. Scratch allows users to program by simply clicking programming code blocks together. It is a dynamic, object-oriented, event-driven language.

Scratch is free to download. It also works and (more importantly) looks the same on Windows, MacOS, and Linux. It comes complete with over 650 sprite images, more than 70 backgrounds, over 80 sound effects and nearly 80 example programs.

The Scratch website is http://scratch.mit.edu. There is a Scratch online community where programmers can share, comment, tag, download and remix programs they write and upload to the site. There are over 600,000 registered members and over 2,500,000 projects have been shared online. You do not have to register to download Scratch, use Scratch, or view the programs others have uploaded online.

Programming Blocks

Scratch uses programming blocks (sometimes called bricks or tiles) to control what happens in the program. Each block has underlying computer code that tells the program what to do in a language it understands (Java). Each block has been grouped with like blocks and painted the same color. For example, all the motion blocks are a dark blue. Each set of blocks can be found in their own "drawer", located in the upper left corner of the program. Usually, the blocks control individual "sprites".

Sprites

A sprite is a graphic element that can be moved as one piece. Sprites can be turned, shrunk, have their color altered, and collisions between sprites can be detected. The default sprite when you open Scratch is the cat, which has two costumes and one sound preloaded. There are several ways to get or modify sprites in Scratch, including drawing your own, importing one of Scratch's, and importing images stored on your computer (making it eay to use almost any online image you find and save).

The Scratch 1.4 Environment

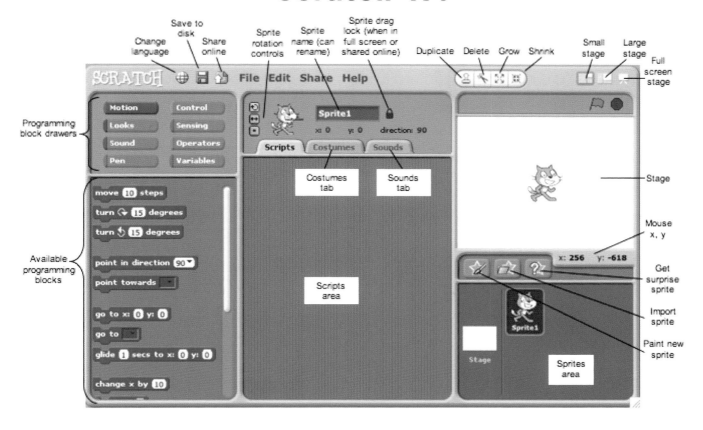

(Educator's Note: I generally print this on a transparency and have students fill in their own blank copy as an introduction to using Scratch.)

Name _____ Per _____ Date _____

Scratch 1.4

SCRATCH

File   Edit   Share   Help

Scripts   Costumes   Sounds

Sprite1
x 0   y 0   direction 90

Motion   Control
Looks   Sensing
Sound   Operators
Pen   Variables

move 10 steps
turn 15 degrees
turn 15 degrees
point in direction 90
point towards
go to x: 0 y: 0
go to
glide 1 secs to x: 0 y: 0
change x by 10

x: 256   Y: -618

Sprite1

Stage

Scratch 1.4 Intro Worksheet

1. What are the 8 "brick drawers" in the upper left corner?

2. What is the top brick called in the (**Sound**) drawer?

3. Which drawer has a brick labeled (**ask<what's your name?> and wait)**?

4. What's another name for the (**Operators**) drawer?

5. How many bricks are in the (**Variables**) drawer?

6. What is the default setting for the (**set pen size to #**) brick?

7. What is the last brick in the (**Control**) drawer?

8. How many graphic effects can you choose between for the (**change <color> effect by <25>)** brick in the (Looks) drawer?

9. What color is the (**Sensing**) drawer?

10. What color is the (**Pen**) drawer?

11. What is the **gray globe** for (upper left)?

12. What does the "**Share**" menu let you do (if you have an account)?

13. Under the "**Help**" menu, what is the copyright date of this program?

14. What do the three **gray/white buttons** in the upper right corner allow you to do?

15. In the middle of the Scratch screen, what does the button with **a star and a question mark** do?

16. How many main folders are within the "**Costumes**" folder?

17. How many **costumes** does the original cat have preloaded?

18. How many **sounds** does the original cat have preloaded?

19. If you select "**File – Open**", how many main folders are in the "Examples" folder?

20. What three options do you have at the top of the "**Costumes**" tab?

Programming Tutorials

1. Using the Paint Editor

1. Click on the "Paint New Sprite" button

2. Create your own person. Use color. Be creative. Have fun.

3. Use the blue Motion drawer and the yellow Control drawer to put together the following code in the Scripts area:

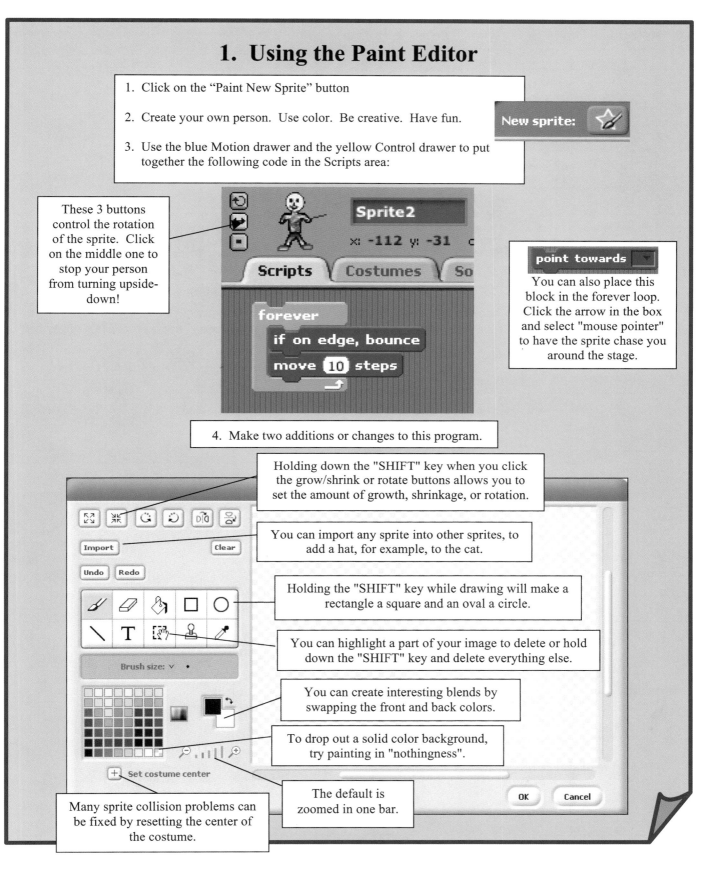

These 3 buttons control the rotation of the sprite. Click on the middle one to stop your person from turning upside-down!

You can also place this block in the forever loop. Click the arrow in the box and select "mouse pointer" to have the sprite chase you around the stage.

4. Make two additions or changes to this program.

Holding down the "SHIFT" key when you click the grow/shrink or rotate buttons allows you to set the amount of growth, shrinkage, or rotation.

You can import any sprite into other sprites, to add a hat, for example, to the cat.

Holding the "SHIFT" key while drawing will make a rectangle a square and an oval a circle.

You can highlight a part of your image to delete or hold down the "SHIFT" key and delete everything else.

You can create interesting blends by swapping the front and back colors.

To drop out a solid color background, try painting in "nothingness".

The default is zoomed in one bar.

Many sprite collision problems can be fixed by resetting the center of the costume.

(Educator's Note: Encourage your students to try out the various settings in the Paint Editor. It is a part of Scratch that is easily worth paying for on its own merit. Show them how to experiment with fills and gradients (a great way to make eyes) and how to change the size of the brush and line tools.)

2. Creating Backgrounds

- Click on the Stage, then the Backgrounds Tab and Edit.
- Create at least three different backgrounds. Some ideas are shown below.

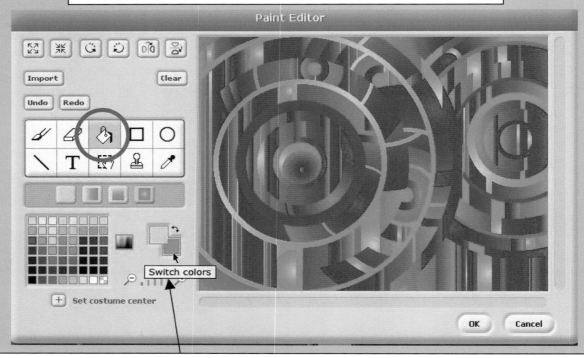

You can get very interesting effects by using the Paint Tool and filling in a blend (or gradient) of two colors.

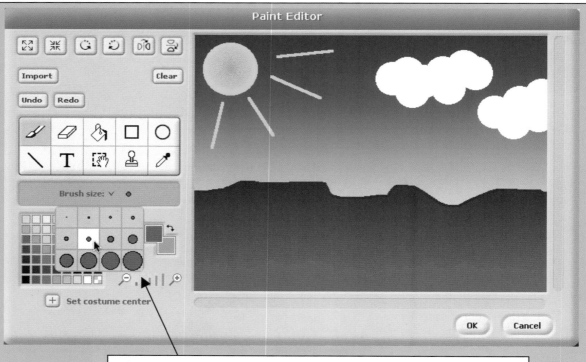

Changing the brush size can also help to add details to your background.

3. Importing Sprites – Artistic Scene

- This is an artistic creation, no programming at all, but it will help familiarize you with importing sprites in Scratch.
- Create a scene using at least 10 sprites and/or backgrounds.
- Look around Scratch's preloaded backgrounds and Sprites to get an overall idea in mind.
- Import your background first, then begin adding sprites. The image below contains 4 people, 2 dogs, and 2 items.
- You can access Scratch's preloaded sprite library (over 650 in all) by clicking on the "Choose new sprite from file" button (it's circled in red below).

You can use the "grow" and "shrink" buttons to fix the size of your sprites.

You can easily change a sprite's direction by clicking on and moving the blue direction pointer as in the image above.

If necessary, you can even edit a sprite (to erase a corner, for instance) by clicking on the "Costumes" tab.

4. Graphic Effects – Crazy Cat

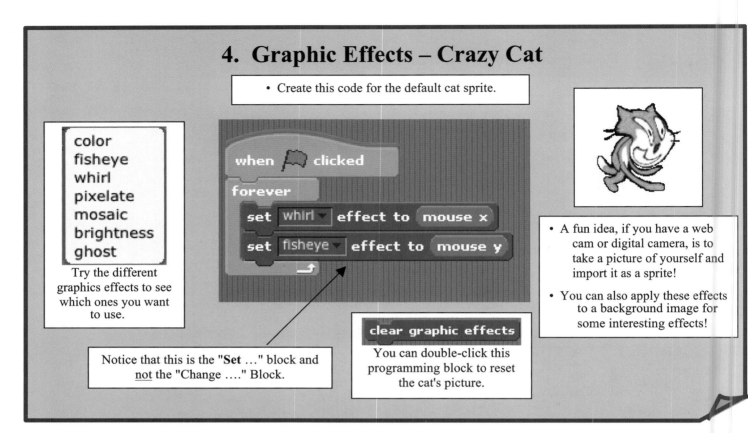

- Create this code for the default cat sprite.

color
fisheye
whirl
pixelate
mosaic
brightness
ghost

Try the different graphics effects to see which ones you want to use.

```
when clicked
forever
    set whirl effect to mouse x
    set fisheye effect to mouse y
```

Notice that this is the "**Set** …" block and <u>not</u> the "Change …." Block.

clear graphic effects

You can double-click this programming block to reset the cat's picture.

- A fun idea, if you have a web cam or digital camera, is to take a picture of yourself and import it as a sprite!
- You can also apply these effects to a background image for some interesting effects!

Scratch uses a Cartesian coordinate system where 0,0 is at the center of the Stage. X and Y increase to the right and up (respectively) and decrease to the left and down (respectively). The Stage measures 480 pixels horizontally (-240 to 240) and 360 pixels vertically (-180 to 180).

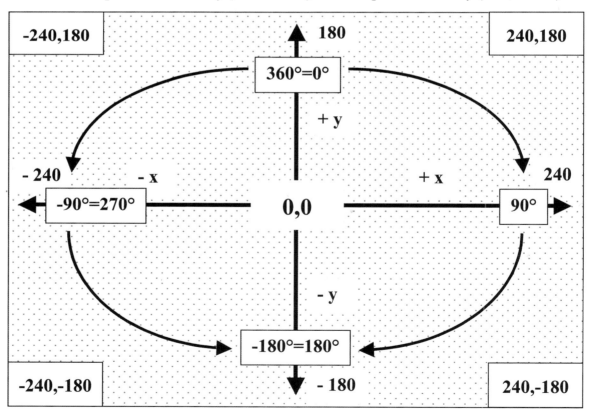

5. Controlling Movement – Three Variations

Create each of these movement programs for a different one, so you don't get any overlapping code on a single sprite

- The usual convention when you are already using the arrow keys is to use the W-A-S-D keys to control movement.

This is the simplest way to control moving. **1**

This method allows control by the four arrow keys, but is a bit "jerky" and slow. **2**

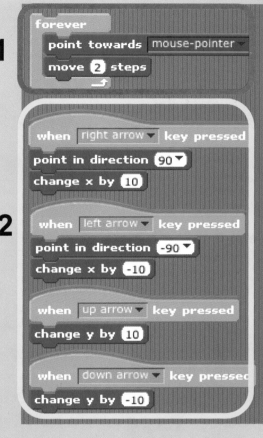

3

Method 3 is the smoothest and most commonly useful way to control movement. Notice that the left and right movements also include a direction to point in.

Look at this quick help coordinate map if you get confused with the directions for up / down / left / right.

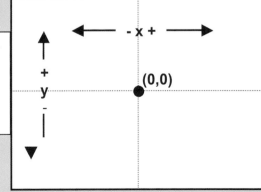

Remember that these 3 buttons control the rotation of the sprite. Click the middle one to stop your sprite from turning upside-down!

6. Changing Costumes – Celebrity Dress Up

1. Find a celebrity image online and import it into the stage background of Scratch (or use a camera to take a picture of yourself!).

2. Erase the background in the paint editor. You can use the eraser tool (changing sizes helps). If the background is a solid color, you can use the paint tool to paint in "transparency" (the grey-white checked color).

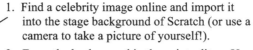

3. Duplicate the entire sprite. (click on the "copy" button or use the stamp tool).

4. Then, right-click on the copied sprite and select "turn into new sprite".

5. Choose a feature to change. The eyes are an easy one to start with. Erase everything except the eyes. (The easy way to do this is to use the select tool to outline the part you want to keep then press Shift-Delete (or Shift-Backspace) to delete everything else!)

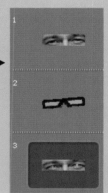

5. Go to "costumes" and copy the image, leaving one "good" image.

6. Change the feature (eye color, nose size, etc) in the copy. You can draw over it or "import" another image from within the Paint Editor to add to it.

7. Build the code shown.

8. Make at least 2 changes to at least 4 features (hair, eyes, nose, ears, mustache).

```
when Sprite2 clicked
next costume
```

Project Notes:
- This is not an assignment to simply graffiti a picture. You should be able to click on the features to return to the original image.
- Neither is this an assignment meant to put down or disparage a celebrity or other students.
- Do not use someone's picture from your class without their permission.
- Do not make the picture gruesome, bloody, or hateful in any way. ☺

7. Changing Costumes – Autobiography Collage

- Create a collage about 6 things that are an important part of your life. Ideas include:
  - your picture, family, pets, hobbies, sports, school
  - favorite movies, books, singers, foods, sports, games
  - colleges you want to attend, places you want to live, or jobs you want to have in the future

- Make two costumes for each. One is a "thumbnail" or small image. When clicked, it should switch to the second costume. This can be a larger image, an image with text, just text, or an alternate image explaining why it is important to you.

FAVORITE QUOTE

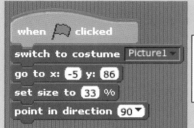

This code sets the original costume, location, size, and direction for each sprite.

This code tells the sprite to…
- go in front of everything else
- switch costumes
- go to the center of the stage (0,0)
- grow to normal size
- wait
- switch back, reset the size and go back to the first location

Shown above are the two costumes for three of the sprites in the example collage.

- You can also make the sprite tilt, spin, talk, change color, etc. to jazz up your presentation.

- You can save time by dragging a script to another sprite. Scratch will copy it over for you!

8. Using Instruments ⁻Making Music

1. Import a sprite and modify it (or draw your own) so that you have two costumes, one "singing" (with the mouth open) and one not singing (with the mouth closed).

2. A handy trick is to press the Shift key when using the rotation button in the Paint Editor. This lets you choose the amount of roation you want when you're rotating the top of the head up to create the "singing" costume.

This command block adds a nice visual effect.

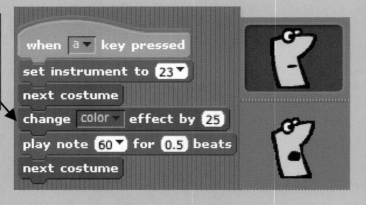

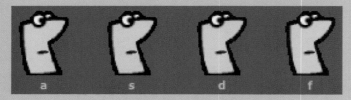

3. After you create your first "singer", duplicate it to copy all the code with it.

4. Change the "when 'a' key pressed" to the next key on the keyboard.

5. It works well to keep the instrument set the same.

6. Change the "play note '60' …" to the next white note on the piano keyboard.

7. Add an insteresting background on the Stage.

There are three ways to make sounds in Scratch:
1. Play an imported sound (114 available)
2. Play a percussion (drum) sound (49 available)
3. Play an instrument sound (128 available)

This program makes use of the instrument sounds. You can find a list of all the available sounds in Appendix B – Music Basics.

9. Drawing Commands – Name Art

- Create a sprite with your first initial. You can "Choose new sprite from file" to get your letters. They are under "Costumes – Letters".
- Make all of the code for your first letter, then duplicate that sprite and change the costume for your other initials.

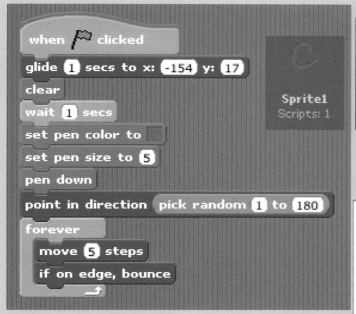

Using the "duplicate" option when you right-click on a sprite also copies all the script from the sprite!

You can "Choose new sprite from file" to get your letters. They are under "Costumes – Letters".

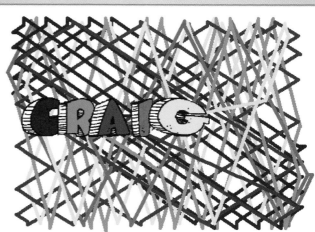

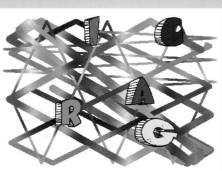

You can get interesting effects by trying some of these command blocks in the "forever" loop.

1. "set pen color to (x position)" = rainbows
2. "set pen size to (abs of (x position))" = blobs
3. "stamp" = interesting lines

You can also save a picture of your name art and even set it as your computer's desktop pattern. To do this, right-click (or control-click) on the stage and select "save picture of stage…".

10. Using Hide and Show – Hidden Objects

1. Choose a background to work with. The one shown is called "room1" from the "Indoors" folder. You can also search online for a "hidden object background".

2. Import pictures to hide around the room (like the baseball). You can also duplicate the original background and cut out an image (like the guitar). You should have at least 10 hidden objects.

3. Add the code. It basically tells the object to show up at the start, blink if clicked on, then disappear. If your objects are only black and white, then they won't change color with this code!

4. Create a variable to count the objects as they are found. The most important part of variable use is that you should always make them "for all sprites", never "for this sprite only".

5. Add the "set found to 0" and "change found by 1" to the hidden items.

6. Create the code that checks to see if all the items have been found. When they are all found (found = 10), one of the hidden items shoud say "All done!!".

Notice that you can change the names from the default "sprite 1" to something more descriptive.

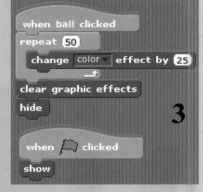

You can also find some good hidden object backgrounds online, like the ones shown here.

11. Using Conditionals   Maze

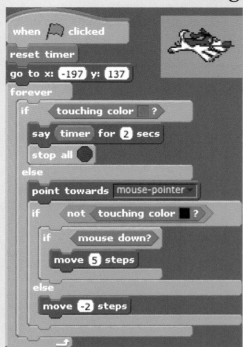

- This program makes use of an interesting conditional statement, the "if ... else" block. Notice that they can also be "nested" within each other to get the desired effect.
- The maze can be drawn as a sprite or on the background.
- The color red is the finish line and the sprite (a dog) will move toward the mouse pointer unless touching the color of the maze lines (black).

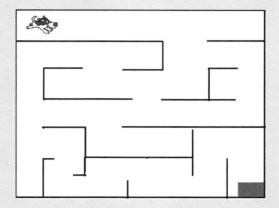

- There is an inherent problem in this type of code, that the moving sprite (the dog) can sometimes walk backwards through the walls of the maze. It helps minimize this problem if you use a round ball instead of the dog (less parts sticking out when it turns around). You can challenge your students to modify the program to fix the problem altogether or point out that it is a cheat for the game.

- Another potential "cheat" is to simply grab the sprite during the game and drag it to the goal. This is not possible in full screen mode if you have the lock closed. Opening the lock makes the sprite draggable both online and I nfull screen mode.

- You can also make the movement controlled by the arrow keys (as shown in Program 5).

- A more advanced idea is to put the movement code on the maze sprite and move the maze around a stationary dog or ball in the middle of the screen. You have to reverse the directions, though, so to move the dog right, the maze would move to the left, to move up it would move down, etc. A side benefit of this idea is that you can make the maze very large (200% so it's off the screen) and it will still move/show all of it during the game.

12. Platform Game

1. Draw a platform as a sprite (<u>not on the stage</u>). Include ladders to climb and edges to drop from. Add a thin layer of another color (I used red) under each platform (this is to make the cat climb when it walks up or down the hills).
2. Make the cat move left – right with the arrow keys.
3. Make the cat climb when pressing up **and** touching a ladder (sprite).
4. Make the cat fall if not touching the platform or ladder.
5. Make the cat move up when touching the color red (or whichever color you used in step 1).

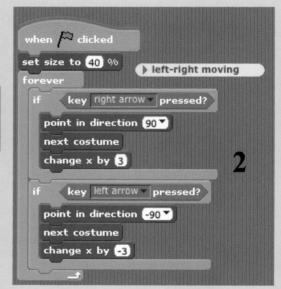

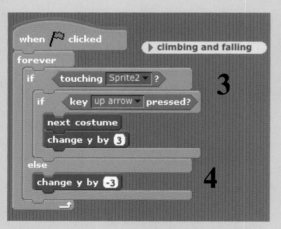

Ideas to improve the game:
- Add a goal to reach or items to "pick up" around the screen
- Duplicate the platform sprite and change the second copy. Have it switch images evey 2-3 seconds – this will simulate disappearing platforms.
- Add a forest background and change the ladders into vines.
- Modify the "up arrow" code so that the cat can jump up, even if not touching the ladders.

13. Simulating Gravity   Jumping Cat

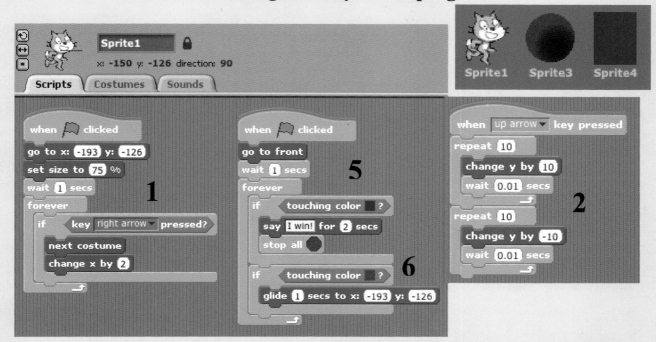

1. Create the code for the cat to start in the lower left corner and move to the right when the right arrow is pressed. You may need to change its size as well.

2. Add the "jumping" code. You can modify the numbers to change the jump. Notice that the "when up arrow key pressed" allows the code to be used over and over without a "forever" loop.

3. Draw a ball. Remember to hold "shift" to make a perfect circle. If you fill it with a two color, circular blend, it will look a little 3D.

4. Add the code to make the ball roll. Notice that we are using "change x by -5" instead of "move -5 steps" so we can make the ball look like it's rolling.

5. Create the finish line (purple block) and add the "I win" code.

6. Finally, add the "if touching color green" code to send the cat back to start if it hits the ball.

14. Asking Questions   Quiz Show

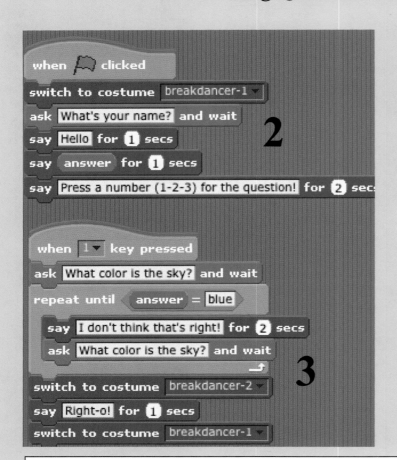

```
when [flag] clicked
switch to costume breakdancer-1 ▾
ask What's your name? and wait
say Hello for 1 secs
say answer for 1 secs
say Press a number (1-2-3) for the question! for 2 secs
```

2

```
when 1 ▾ key pressed
ask What color is the sky? and wait
repeat until  answer = blue
    say I don't think that's right! for 2 secs
    ask What color is the sky? and wait
switch to costume breakdancer-2 ▾
say Right-o! for 1 secs
switch to costume breakdancer-1 ▾
```

3

1. Start by importing the "breakdancer". You will need his other 3 costumes, so go ahead and import them, too. Make sure you put them all on the same sprite.
2. Build the intro code. Notice that you can put the "answer" variable into the "say" code block.
3. Build the code for question 1. (You can import a number 1 sprite if you want – I colored mine in red - but the code needs to stay on the breakdancer.)
4. Duplicate the question code to create numbers 2 and 3 (right-click or control-click on the top code block to duplicate). Notice that you can use an "or" block to check for two similar answers.
5. Have the breakdancer change to a different costume for each different question.

4

```
when 2 ▾ key pressed
ask Who was our 1st President? and wait
repeat until  answer = George Washington or answer = Washington
    say I don't think that's right! for 2 secs
```

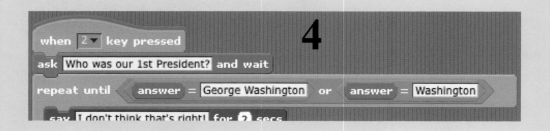

15. Pong

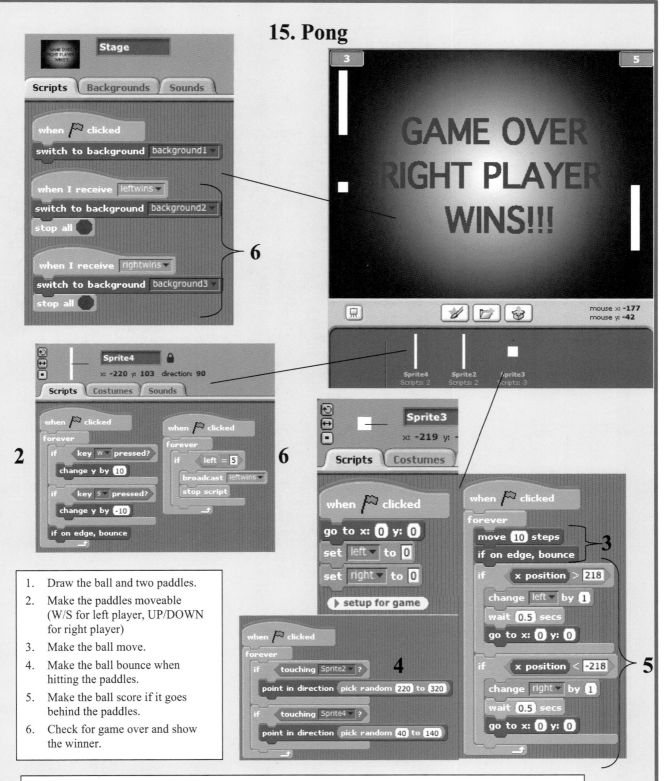

1. Draw the ball and two paddles.
2. Make the paddles moveable (W/S for left player, UP/DOWN for right player)
3. Make the ball move.
4. Make the ball bounce when hitting the paddles.
5. Make the ball score if it goes behind the paddles.
6. Check for game over and show the winner.

Ideas to improve the game:
- Add a sound when the ball is hit and/or missed.
- Use a separate sprite with costumes to show the score (the numbers 1, 2, 3, 4etc.)
- Add a special move button for each player that speeds up / slows down the ball or makes it change direction in mid-flight.

16. Using a Missile – Hit the Target

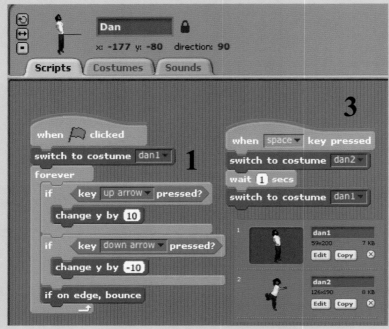

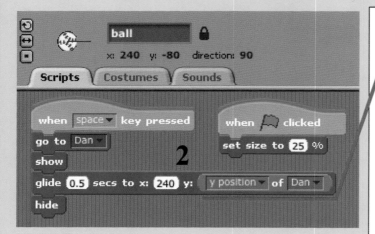

1. Import the two "Dan" costumes. Make him move up and down with the arrow keys.

2. Import the ball. When the space key is pressed, make it go to Dan, appear, and fly across the screen. Use the "y position of Dan" block from the Sensing palette so that the ball flies straight across the screen from whichever height Dan is curently at.

3. Make Dan switch costumes when the ball is "thrown" (the "space" key is pressed).

4. Draw a target. It's basically a large red oval around a smaller red oval with white painted in between. The key idea here is to **set its rotation to "don't rotate"** – the square button – so that it doesn't turn sideways when it bounces up and down.

5. Make it point up initially and then move up and down forever.

6. Add in a "if touching ball" code block to see when it gets hit. You'll need to import the "FingerSnap" sound. Notice that this stops the target from moving when it gets hit because it is in the same loop as the movement code.

Ideas to improve the game:
- Add a background
- Add a score (place the "change score by 1" variable block in the "if touching ball" loop)
- Make the target "explode" when hit by switching costumes
- Add an extra target
- Add blocking pieces that also move up and down to shield the target.
- Make this a "themed" game – inport sprites from online for Star Wars, Sponge Bob, Transformers, etc.

17. Intermediate Art – Recreate a Landscape

1. Choose a landscape image to recreate using Scratch's Paint Editor. You can find 10 free landscapes at **http://bit.ly/I2Vyrg** (capitalization counts!) or you can search for your own online using the search terms "free landscape background".

2. Import the original landscape image as the background and paint your image as a second background.

3. Use the code shown to switch between the two as you work (you can also open the original image and view it side-by-side as you paint in Scratch).

4. Your landscape should recreate the basic colors, shapes, shadows and (when possible) textures of the original image. The amount of detail you include is up to you, but you will find different paintbrush sizes and using blended (or gradient) fills extremely useful.

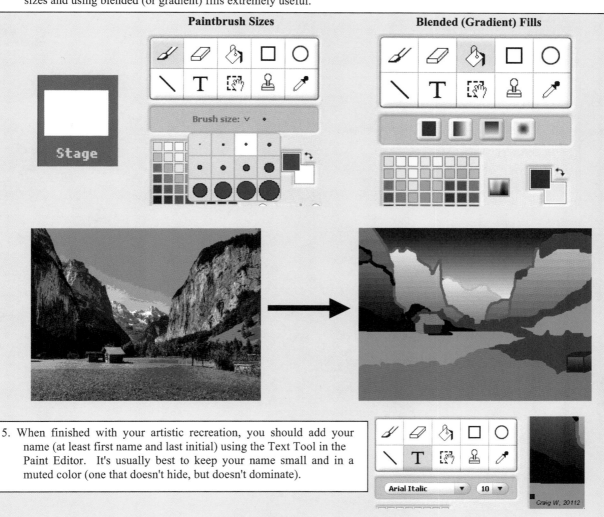

5. When finished with your artistic recreation, you should add your name (at least first name and last initial) using the Text Tool in the Paint Editor. It's usually best to keep your name small and in a muted color (one that doesn't hide, but doesn't dominate).

6. Finally, save a picture of your artwork by right-clicking (or control-clicking) on the stage and choosing "save picture of stage..."). You can also print this saved image from any image preview program.

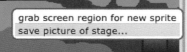

18. Asteroids

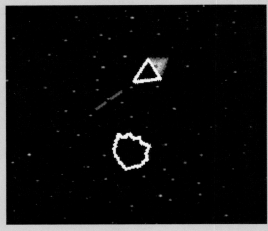

1. Start by drawing the 3 ship views.
2. Add the movement codes.
3. Create the "laser". When the fire key is pressed, it should go to the ship, point in the direction the ship is headed, show up and move until it hits the edge or the asteroid.
4. Create the 2 views of the asteroid.
5. Make the asteroid show up in a random position, point in a random direction, move around the stage until it hits the ship or is hit by the laser.
6. Add in the ship firing thrusters and blowing up.
7. Additional ideas are to add sounds, more asteroids, more lasers, a black hole, an enemy ship, etc.

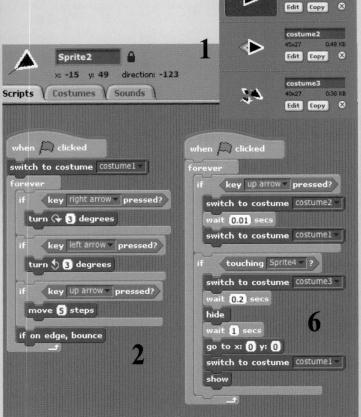

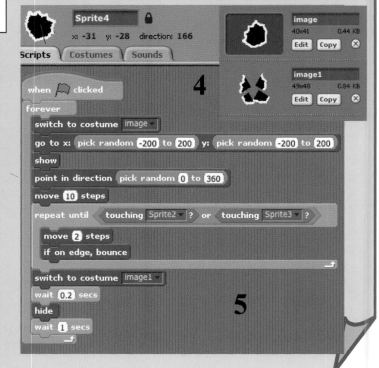

19. Using Animated Gifs – Target Shooting

Gifs are one of the most popular image formats online. Animated gifs contain more than one image and switch between them in a loop, creating the illusion of a small movie.

1. Download this animated gif (**http://bit.ly/He2wLU** capitalizaion counts!) or find another online.

2. Import it from the costumes tab of a pre-existing sprite (like the cat). This way it will load in all of the costumes associated with it.

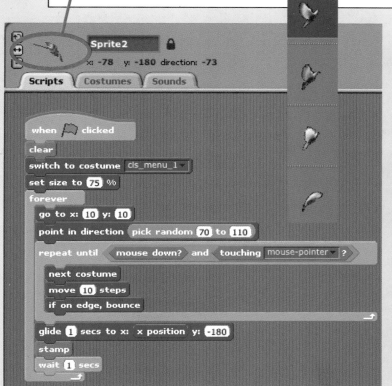

For Scratch, animated gifs are treated as separate costumes, but <u>they must be imported from the "costumes" tab</u>. Importing from the "Choose new sprite from file" button will only import the first costume.

20. Using Layers – Sniper Game

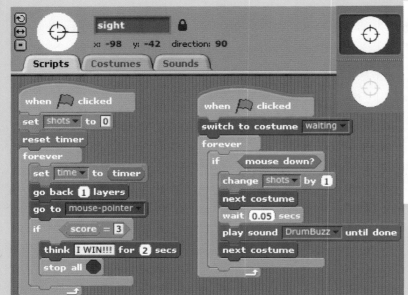

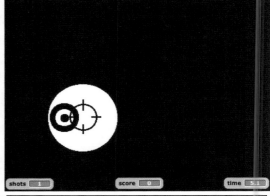

There are three layers to this program: the black targets in front of the white sight with the black background in back. The key programming block is the "go back 1 layers" block in the sight code that keeps it behind the targets so you can see them.

There are a total of four sprites, but the three targets are all the same. Make the first target the way you want, then duplicate it to get the others.

Key Block

This block keeps the "sight" always behind the targets, letting the black targets show on the white circle behind them.

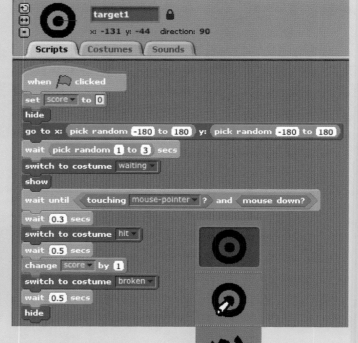

21. Using Instruments – Create-a-Song

Scratch allows both instrument and drum (percussion) sounds. Ths instruments are accessed by first setting the instrument and then playing a note for a number of beats. Appendix B contains a list of the instrument and drum types available. Most music that we commonly hear today is played with four (4) beats per measure. So a normal length for a note would be 1 beat – the higher the number, the longer the note is held.

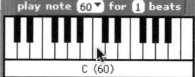

```
set instrument to 1 ▼
play note 60 ▼ for 0.5 beats
```

You may also find it helpful to change the tempo (or speed) of the song. The default tempo is 60 bpm (beats per minute) which makes 1 beat last for 1 second. The higher the tempo, the shorter the length of each beat and the faster the song.

```
set tempo to 60 bpm
```

Here are some example songs to program. See which ones you recognize!

```
when a ▼ key pressed
set tempo to 80 bpm
set instrument to 57 ▼
play note 60 ▼ for 1 beats
play note 67 ▼ for 1 beats
play note 65 ▼ for 0.3 beats
play note 64 ▼ for 0.3 beats
play note 62 ▼ for 0.3 beats
play note 72 ▼ for 1 beats
play note 60 ▼ for 1 beats
play note 65 ▼ for 0.3 beats
play note 64 ▼ for 0.3 beats
play note 62 ▼ for 0.3 beats
play note 72 ▼ for 1 beats
play note 60 ▼ for 1 beats
play note 65 ▼ for 0.3 beats
play note 64 ▼ for 0.3 beats
play note 65 ▼ for 0.3 beats
play note 62 ▼ for 2 beats
```

```
when b ▼ key pressed
set tempo to 60 bpm
set instrument to 36 ▼
play note 69 ▼ for 0.3 beats
rest for 0.2 beats
play note 62 ▼ for 0.3 beats
rest for 0.5 beats
play note 72 ▼ for 0.3 beats
rest for 0.15 beats
play note 69 ▼ for 0.2 beats
rest for 0.08 beats
play note 67 ▼ for 0.3 beats
rest for 0.2 beats
play note 60 ▼ for 0.3 beats
rest for 0.2 beats
```

```
when c ▼ key pressed
set tempo to 100 bpm
set instrument to 57 ▼
play note 65 ▼ for 1 beats
play note 62 ▼ for 0.5 beats
play note 58 ▼ for 1 beats
play note 62 ▼ for 1 beats
play note 65 ▼ for 1 beats
play note 70 ▼ for 2 beats
```

```
when d ▼ key pressed
set tempo to 100 bpm
set instrument to 20 ▼
play note 72 ▼ for 1.25 beats
play note 71 ▼ for 1 beats
play note 69 ▼ for 0.5 beats
play note 67 ▼ for 2 beats
play note 65 ▼ for 0.75 beats
play note 64 ▼ for 1.5 beats
play note 62 ▼ for 1.5 beats
play note 60 ▼ for 2 beats
```

- Program a song that you know.
  (You can also finish one of the examples that are started above).

22. Pac-Man

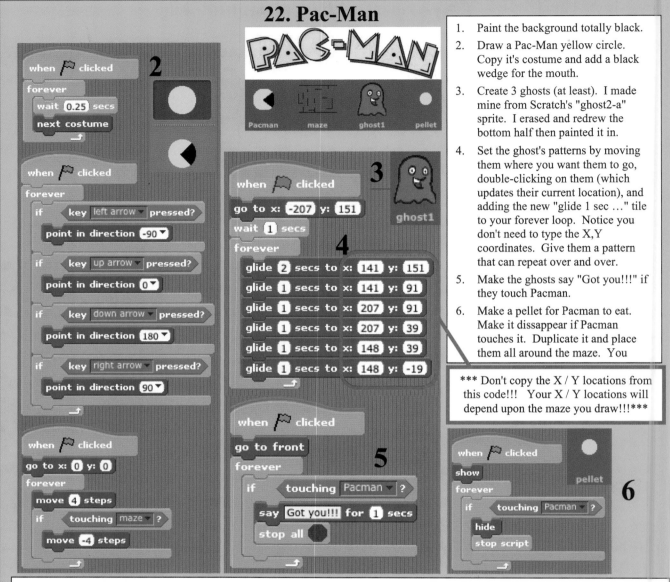

1. Paint the background totally black.

2. Draw a Pac-Man yellow circle. Copy it's costume and add a black wedge for the mouth.

3. Create 3 ghosts (at least). I made mine from Scratch's "ghost2-a" sprite. I erased and redrew the bottom half then painted it in.

4. Set the ghost's patterns by moving them where you want them to go, double-clicking on them (which updates their current location), and adding the new "glide 1 sec ..." tile to your forever loop. Notice you don't need to type the X,Y coordinates. Give them a pattern that can repeat over and over.

5. Make the ghosts say "Got you!!!" if they touch Pacman.

6. Make a pellet for Pacman to eat. Make it dissappear if Pacman touches it. Duplicate it and place them all around the maze. You

*** Don't copy the X / Y locations from this code!!! Your X / Y locations will depend upon the maze you draw!!!***

Some important notes:
(1) The maze should be a separate sprite, not drawn onto the background.

(2) The center of the maze should be transparent, not a black "fill" – the background should be black and it will show through.

(3) You can hold down the Shift key when drawing a line to make it straight (the line tool, not the paintbrush tool). You can also press the caps-lock key to keep it set on "straight" all the time!

(4) Your ghosts' pattern will depend on your maze, so you can't just copy the numbers in the "glide 1 secs to ..." shown above!

(5) If your ghost is moving a long ways, consider changing the "1" to a "2" in the "glide 1 secs ..." – this will keep it from suddenly speeding up as it moves through its pattern.

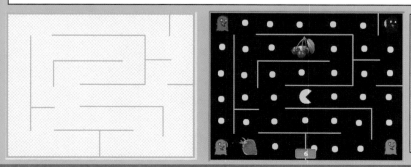

Extra Challenge Ideas
- Make a score
- Add Pacman sounds
- Add "power pellets" so Pacman can eat the ghosts
- Make a "pass thru" tunnel on the sides
- Make it a two-player game
- Make fruit appear randomly for extra points
- Make a 2nd level when you eat all the pellets

23. Using Scrolling Backgrounds – Cat Walk

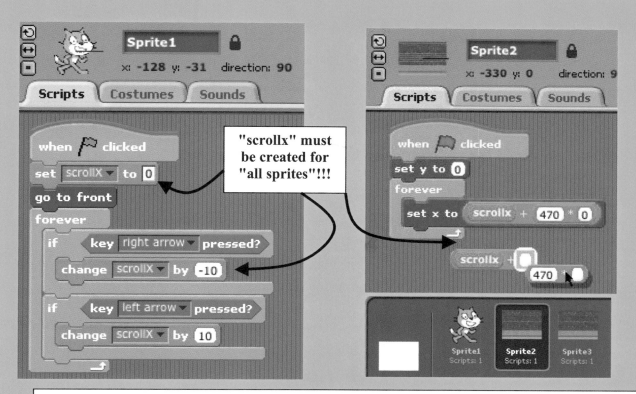

- Though this seems like very simple programming code, it is easy to mess up!!
- Notice that the variable (scrollx) changes in the **opposite direction** from the arrow key being pressed. The movement of the background creates the impression of movement by the cat, even though the cat never actually moves.
- You will need several "walls" (or whatever background you choose). Each should be set to "(scrollx) + (470) * (**0**)", then "(scrollx) + (470) * (**1**)", then "(scrollx) + (470) * (**2**)", etc.
- You may need to adjust the "470" ot a lower or higher number to reduce flickering at the edges.
- The "(470) * (0)" has to go **into** the "(scrollx) + ( )" or the math won't work correctly.
- You can increase the realism of the scrolling by flipping each other background sprite horizontally so their edges match up more closely.
- Finally, make a few additions. Make the cat change costumes to walk, add jumping, create a finish line, make some objects to avoid, add a timer, create a static stage background and just scroll the lower half of the foreground. Have some fun with this!!

24. Simulating 3D – Desert Walk

1. Import or create a background on the stage.
2. Make a copy of that background.
3. Press the "Edit" button on the copy.
4. From the Paint Editor, "Import" an object that you want to work with. **DO NOT click off of the imported object.**
5. Use the shrink or grow buttons to change the object's size. Place it near the center of the background, off on the right-hand side.
6. Make another copy of the original background.
7. Again, Import the same object and use the grow button to make it larger.
8. Place the object a little more down on the background and a little more to the right than the last object.
9. Continue this process (copy – import – grow – place) until you have 6-10 different backgrounds for the stage.
10. Create the codes shown above.

25. Using the Pen Commands – Etch-a-Sketch Art

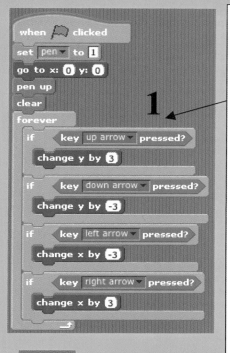

1

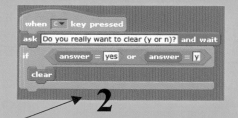

2

There are 6 basic ideas in this program: movement, pen color, pen size, pen up/down, background color, and clearing the screen.

1. Movement is controlled by the arrow keys.
2. 'c' asks if they want to clear the screen
3. The line colors can be changed by pressing a key (r-o-y-g-b-i-v-l-w-p-n).
4. The 'h' key shows this list.
5. The space key toggles the pen up (-1) or down (1) by multiplying the variable "pen" by -1.
6. 'a' and 'z' make the pen wider or narrower, respectively. The pen width can't go below 1.
7. The 'x' key changes between 11 colors of stage backgrounds.

3

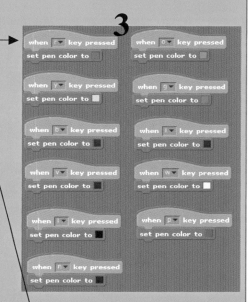

7

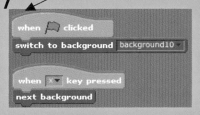

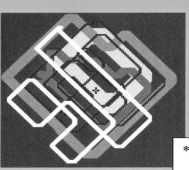

5

6

r-o-y-g-b-i-v-l-w-p-n

* This is a separate sprite, made with the text tool.

4

** You can save a picture of your artwork by right-clicking on the screen (Ctrl-click if you don't have a right-mouse button) and select "save picture of stage".

26. Using Lists – Number Guessing Game

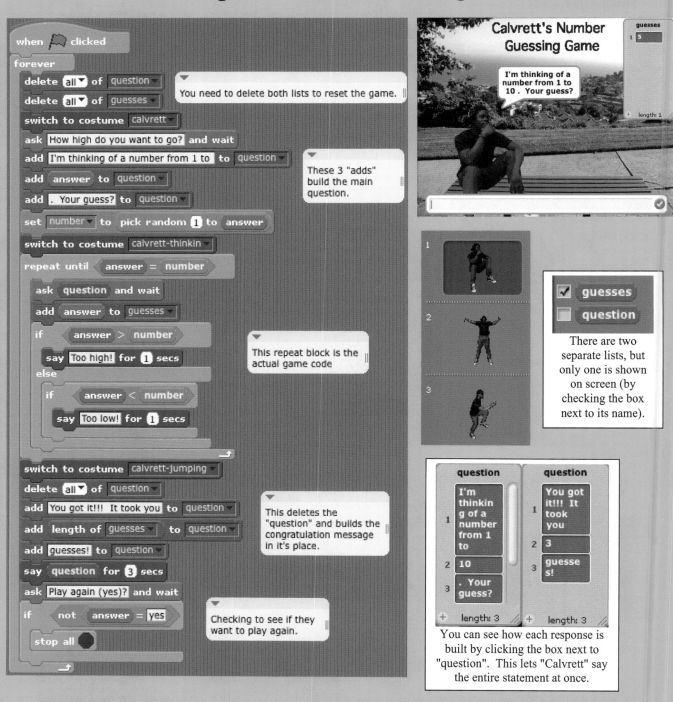

when clicked
forever
  delete all of question
  delete all of guesses
      You need to delete both lists to reset the game.
  switch to costume calvrett
  ask How high do you want to go? and wait
  add I'm thinking of a number from 1 to to question
  add answer to question
  add . Your guess? to question
      These 3 "adds" build the main question.
  set number to pick random 1 to answer
  switch to costume calvrett-thinkin
  repeat until answer = number
    ask question and wait
    add answer to guesses
    if answer > number
      say Too high! for 1 secs
    else
      if answer < number
        say Too low! for 1 secs

This repeat block is the actual game code

  switch to costume calvrett-jumping
  delete all of question
  add You got it!!! It took you to question
  add length of guesses to question
  add guesses! to question
  say question for 3 secs
  ask Play again (yes)? and wait
  if not answer = yes
    stop all

This deletes the "question" and builds the congratulation message in it's place.

Checking to see if they want to play again.

Calvrett's Number Guessing Game

I'm thinking of a number from 1 to 10 . Your guess?

guesses
1 5
length: 1

☑ guesses
☐ question

There are two separate lists, but only one is shown on screen (by checking the box next to its name).

question	question
1 I'm thinking of a number from 1 to	1 You got it!!! It took you
2 10	2 3
3 . Your guess?	3 guesses!
length: 3	length: 3

You can see how each response is built by clicking the box next to "question". This lets "Calvrett" say the entire statement at once.

- You don't have to use "Calvrett" for the questioner – you could use a picture of your face with different "thoughtful" expressions.
- This program makes use of several different "key blocks": asking questions, making lists, making a variable, random numbers, and conditional checking (if… loops).
- I would start with the actual game code (in the middle of the program) then add the lists once it is working correctly.

27. Create Your Own Retro Game

Recreate a famous retro game ("retro" meaning from the recent past). You may use online images and sounds. Your game does not have to recreate the entire original game, but it should closely approximate the original game play. This should be your programming entirely and not simply someone else's work that you modify. Fill in the "Retro Game Planning" page and get the teacher's approval before you start programming. Have fun!!

15 Suggested "Retro" Games to Program

1. Adventure
2. Breakout
3. DigDug
4. DonkeyKong
5. Duck Hunt

6. Frogger
7. Galaga
8. Jungle Hunt
9. Mario Brothers
10. Missile Command

11. Moon Patrol
12. Pitfall
13. Pole Position
14. Space Invaders
15. Tron (Light Cycles)

Some of these games can be viewed/played online at www.classicgamesarcade.com.

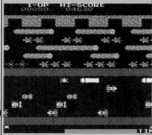
Frogger © Sega,
image from Wikipedia

Free Online Resources

Free Sound Clips and Music Loops
http://www.partnersinrhyme.com

Free Older Game Images
http://www.retrogamezone.co.uk/

Free Animated Gifs
http://www.gifs.net/gif/
http://www.amazing-animations.com
http://www.gifanimations.com/

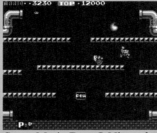
Super Mario Bros © Nintendo,
image from Wikipedia

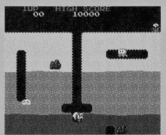
DigDug © Atari,
image from Wikipedia

Space Invaders © Midway,
image from Wikipedia

Pole Position © Atari,
image from Wikipedia

Breakout © Atari,
image from Wikipedia

Making these types of games is a great way to challenge students to program on their own but still give them established guidelines. By using a retro game they already have an idea of what the game should look like and how it should be played. Additionally, most older games have relatively simple gameplay and use 2D interfaces. Another good suggestion is to have them search for "screenshot" and the name of the game to find the backgrounds they need (if they don't want to make their own). Also, if a game is very complex, I usually let the students create just a part of it if necessary. This assignment usually takes 7-8 class days of work time.

28. Create Your Own Original Game

Create your own game. This may be based on another game, but it should not be exactly like another game. You may use online images and sounds or ones that you draw in Scratch. This should be your own planning and programming <u>entirely</u> and not simply someone else's programming that you modify. Fill in the "Original Game Planning" page and get the teacher's approval before you start programming. Have fun!!

The Seven Stages of Game Programming

Stage 1 Vision – get an idea in mind, don't start off too grand just keep it simple. (Sometimes the simplest games are the best!) Don't get bogged down in details (yet). Think of basic questions like will it go side-to-side, up and down, or just down?

Stage 2 Planning – make a list, a web diagram, and/or a drawing about your game idea. What What sprites will you need? Will you need to use any variables? What is the best way for the player to input control?

Stage 3 Programming – start filling in the code for each sprite. Save often and save as different versions (ie. game1, game2) in case you program yourself into a corner and want to go back. It helps to play and fix as you go. Remember to keep variables informative so you can easily remember what they stand for.

Stage 4 Evaluation – step back, play it, think about it again. Do you need to make it faster or slower? Is there an easier way to code it? Will the game make sense to someone else?

Stage 5 Outside Critique – have a friend play and get their opinion. Even though it's difficult, listen to them, listen to them, listen to them. What makes sense to you may be confusing to them!

Stage 6 Repeat Stages 3 through 5 until you are satisfied with your game.

Stage 7 Clean Up – add credits to your game and a Splash Screen to the start or end. Cleanup any cumbersome code. Rename the file with an interesting Game Title.

PPPPP

There is an old saying that really holds true in programming: Prior Planning Prevents Poor Performance. The more you plan out ahead of time, the less problems you will deal with during programming which means you will usually finish your game much more quickly and it will turn out more the way you want it. Since there are usually several ways to program the same thing, the structure or shape of your programming can set you up for an elegant game or a waste of code. I usually write out my ideas on paper first, then start coding on the computer after I have a broad picture. Whichever method you find works best for you remember, prior planning prevents poor performance. (It's even an example of alliteration, for your English language development!)

29. Real-World Challenge #1 – Office Security Lighting

Your programming company has been contacted by another company. They want you to design a computer program to help increase their office security by tying a series of lights to various doors. Their requirements are listed below. You can find their office diagram on the following webpage: `http://bit.ly/HKJASr` (capital letters count). Create a program in Scratch that satisfies their requirements.

Customer Requirements:
1. Green Light in Private Office to come on if the front door opens.
2. Yellow Light outside of Conference Room to come on if Conference Room door is closed.
3. Red Light in Reception to come on if the Private Office door closes.
4. Blue Light in Reception to come on if the Storage & Filing room door opens.
5. A buzzer to sound when the front door opens.
6. Add a push button on the reception desk to disable the security lights and buzzers.

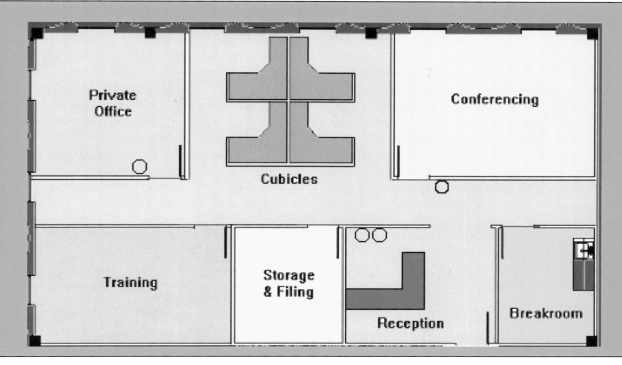

Programming Strategy:
a. Make the doors for each room "movable" (open – close) when clicked on.
b. Tie the required doors to the lights. Make sure you use the colors they requested.
c. Make the front door and Storage & Filing door self-closing (open, wait, then close on it's own).
d. Tie in a buzzer sound to the front door opening.

30. Real World Challenge #2   Debugging Bug Bounce

"When you get a first **entry-level programming** job you will most likely **not** be writing all new code yourself, but instead you will be **modifying and debugging existing code** (program maintenance). The only new code you might write is to make product enhancements to existing products. No one is going to sit you down at a computer and expect you to write an entirely new program all by yourself." ~ posted 6/23/11 by 'Ancient Dragon', a retired programmer at http://www.daniweb.com/software-development/cpp/threads/369511/1588290#post1588290

You have just been hired at a company that specializes in making games for children about bugs. Your first assignment is to debug ☺ an older program (called 'Bug Bounce') that they have received several complaints about. If you can't find and correct the errors in the programming code, they will have to pull the game from their website and issue refunds to all the families that have already purchased it!

The original vision for the game was to control a bug (butterfly) with the right and left arrow keys, making it fly back and forth along the blue / purple boundary, bouncing colored, bouncy balls off of its back until it reached a score of 20 when a "YOU WIN" message shows up. When the bug missed a bouncy ball, it was supposed to subtract from the score and make a laughing sound.

Download the program from **http://bit.ly/Gm2G2f** (capitilization counts!) or recreate it from the code shown. Run it and fix the 10 errors in the coding to address the top 10 complaints that have been received from irate parents.

Top 10 Complaints

1. Bug is flying too high
2. Bug goes up when I press right and down when I press left
3. Bug is not flapping it's wings
4. Bug sometimes goes off the screen
5. One of the bouncy balls stays on the bottom and won't bounce
6. One of the bouncy balls is "frozen" at the top
7. Score doesn't start over with each new game
8. One of the bounce sounds happens even if I don't hit the bouncy ball
9. I don't win when score gets to 20
10. The laughing sound is mean when I miss a bouncy ball

Additional Worksheets

Scratch Reflection Sheet for _____

1. What was the most difficult part about this program?

2. What was the most fun or enjoyable part about this program?

3. Which programming block(s) was (were) the most critical to making the program function correctly?

4. What is one change or addition you made to the basic program you were given?

5. On the following scale, how difficult $1 - 2 - 3 - 4 - 5 - 6 - 7 - 8 - 9 - 10$
   was it to create this program: most   medium   most
                                               easy   difficult

---

Scratch Reflection Sheet for _____

1. What was the most difficult part about this program?

2. What was the most fun or enjoyable part about this program?

3. Which programming block(s) was (were) the most critical to making the program function correctly?

4. What is one change or addition you made to the basic program you were given?

5. On the following scale, how difficult $1 - 2 - 3 - 4 - 5 - 6 - 7 - 8 - 9 - 10$
   was it to create this program: most   medium   most
                                               easy   difficult

Scratch Retro Game Planning

Recreate a retro game. You may use online images and sounds. Your game does not have to recreate the entire original game, but it should closely approximate the original game play. This should be your programming entirely and not simply someone else's work that you modify. Have fun!!

Game Planning Sheet

Type of Game

Breakout	Dig-Dug	DonkeyKong	Frogger	Galaga
Jungle Hunt	Mario Brothers	Missle Command	Pole Position	Space Invaders

Type of Control   mouse pointer   keyboard   arrow-keys

Goal of Game   "You must ... _____

_____

_____

Sprite Images You Will Need from Online   **Teacher's Initials** [ ]

Sketch of Game Screen

Scratch Retro Game Review

1. Title of your game: _____

2. How difficult was it to program your game?   1 – 2 – 3 – 4 – 5 – 6 – 7 – 8 – 9 – 10
                                                   easy   okay   my brain hurts

3. How much is your game like the original?   1 – 2 – 3 – 4 – 5 – 6 – 7 – 8 – 9 – 10
                                                not at all   a little   exactly

4. What was the most challenging part of the programming for your game?

5. Did you draw your sprites on your own, use the Scratch ones or download them from the Internet?

6. If you were to start programming your game over, what would you do differently from the beginning?

Have someone else fill in the bottom portion of this review.

7. Game Reviewer First Name: _____

8. How **fun** was it to play this game?   1 – 2 – 3 – 4 – 5 – 6 – 7 – 8 – 9 – 10
                                             yawn   a little   Woohoo!

9. How **easy** was it to play this game?   1 – 2 – 3 – 4 – 5 – 6 – 7 – 8 – 9 – 10
                                              too easy   just right   too difficult

10. What is one positive comment you can make about this game?

11. What are two things you'd like to see changed about this game?

_____
(Game Reviewer Signature)

Scratch Original Game Planning

Create your own game. This may be based on another game, but it should not be exactly like another game. You may use online images and sounds. This should be your own planning and programming entirely and not simply someone else's work that you modify. Have fun!!

Game Planning Sheet

Goal of Game   "You must ... _____

_____

Type of Game

Animation / Story	Pseudo-3D	Art	Flying / Driving	Shooting
Scrolling	Platform	Sports	Quiz Game	_____

Type of Control   mouse pointer   keyboard   arrow-keys

Sprite Images You Will Need from Online

Teacher's Initials [ ]

Sketch of Game Screen

Scratch Original Game Report

Title of game / story _____

Goal of game / Plot of story _____

_____

_____

Do you have a Start Screen?   YES - NO

Number of …

      sprites:

      stage backgrounds:

      sounds:

      variables (including timer):

Can the user control the game / story? YES - NO   If YES, how? _____

_____

Which sprites did you get from the Internet?

Which sprites did you draw on your own?

How does the game / story end? _____

_____

What is the most interesting part of your game / story?

List 5 important control blocks you used in this program:

Have another person review your game / story

      Reviewer's Name _____

      What is one thing you liked about this game / story:

      What is one thing you like to see added to this game / story:

      On a scale of 5 to 10, how much do you like this game?

                        5 – 6 – 7 – 8 – 9 – 10

                  not bad   greatest game ever

NAME _____

Scratch Online Program Review

WEBSITE: **scratch.mit.edu**

1 Name of Game / Program:
Describe the Program:

Ease of Play (1-hard to 10-easy):

What are two things you like:

What are two things you would change:

What are two programming blocks (tiles) you think they used to create this program:

2 Name of Game / Program:
Describe the Program:

Ease of Play (1-hard to 10-easy):

What are two things you like:

What are two things you would change:

What are two programming blocks (tiles) you think they used to create this program:

3 Name of Game / Program:
Describe the Program:

Ease of Play (1-hard to 10-easy):

What are two things you like:

What are two things you would change:

What are two programming blocks (tiles) you think they used to create this program:

Circle your favorite of the three above.

NAME _____ PER ____ DATE _____

SCRATCH COMMANDS CROSSWORD

Across

1. moves the sprite up
2. moves the sprite to the right
3. draws a line behind the sprite

7. keeps the sprite from moving off the stage
10. checks to see if the sprite is touching a certain color
13. makes the sprite grow larger
14. switches to the next drawing of the sprite

15. chooses a random number
16. points the sprite at the pointer
17. shows the counting timer on the stage
18. sends a message to all sprites
19. loops the enclosed commands forever
20. ends the program

Down

1. sets all graphics effects to 0
4. waits until a broadcast happens
5. hides the sprite
6. pauses the program for 1 second
8. moves the sprite forward
9. plays a sound
11. shows the sprite saying hello
12. checks to see if the space key is pressed

Code blocks:

timer
move 10 steps
stop all
pen down
point towards ▼
next costume
play sound
pick random 1 to 10
clear graphic effects
change size by 10
wait 1 secs
hide
change y by 10
touching color ?
broadcast ▼
say Hello for 2 secs

if on edge, bounce
change x by 10
key space ▼ pressed?
when I receive ▼
forever

(Use the code blocks above to fill in the crossword.)

Appendices

Appendix A – The Coordinate System in Scratch

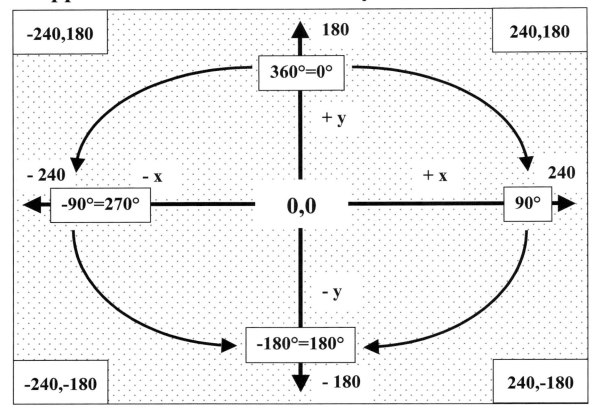

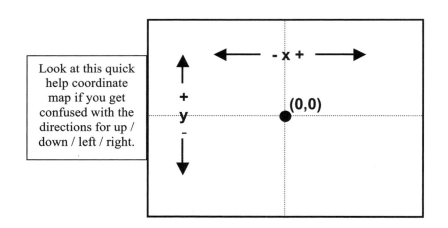

Look at this quick help coordinate map if you get confused with the directions for up / down / left / right.

Appendix B – Music Basics

Modern music is based on scales, a set of 8 notes. The first note is often called the key of the song. The simplest key is C major (sometimes just called C) that starts at middle C (60) and goes up to the next higher C (72). Below is the scale:

C (60) – D (62) – E (64) – F (65) – G (67) – A (69) – B (71) – C (72)

You may notice that the numbers don't change by 2 every time – that is because of the way a major scale is built. The formula for a major scale is 2 whole steps, one ½ , 3 whole steps, one ½. Scratch uses 1 step in place of the ½ steps, so the numbering works out to 2-2-1-2-2-2-1 instead of 1-1-½-1-1-1-½.

2 whole steps – 60 to 62 to 64
1 half step – 64 to 65
3 whole steps – 65 to 67 to 69 to 71
1 half step – 71 to 72

The distance from C (60) to C (72) is known as an octave (a complete jump of eight notes in a scale).

The nice thing about the key of C is that on the piano keyboard you don't have to use any of the black keys (sharps/flats), only the white ones.

Instruments in Scratch

				Percussion
1 – Acoustic Grand	36 – Fretless Bass	71 – Bassoon	106 – Banjo	47 – Low-Mid Tom
2 – Bright Acoustic	37 – Slap Bass 1	72 – Clarinet	107 – Shamisen	48 – Hi-Mid Tom
3 – Electric Grand	38 – Slap Bass 2	73 – Piccolo	108 – Koto	49 – Crash Cymbal 1
4 – Honky-Tonk	39 – Synth Bass 1	74 – Flute	109 – Kalimba	50 – High Tom
5 – Electric Piano 1	40 – Synth Bass 2	75 – Recorder	110 – Bagpipe	51 – Ride Cymbal 1
6 – Electric Piano 2	41 – Violin	76 – Pan Flute	111 – Fiddle	52 – Chinese Cymbal
7 – Harpsichord	42 – Viola	77 – Blown Bottle	112 – Shanai	53 – Ride Bell
8 – Clavinet	43 – Cello	78 – Shakuhachi	113 – Tinkle Bell	54 – Tambourine
9 – Celesta	44 – Contrabass	79 – Whistle	114 – Agogo	55 – Splash Cymbal
10 – Glockenspiel	45 – Tremolo Strings	80 – Ocarina	115 – Steel Drums	56 – Cowbell
11 – Music Box	46 – Pizzicato Strings	81 – Lead 1 (square)	116 – Woodblock	57 – Crash Cymbal 2
12 – Vibraphone	47 – Orchestral Strings	82 – Lead 2 (sawtooth)	117 – Taiko Drum	58 – Vibraslap
13 – Marimba	48 – Timpani	83 – Lead 3 (calliope)	118 – Melodic Tom	59 – Ride Cymbal 2
14 – Xylophone	49 – String Ensemble 1	84 – Lead 4 (chiff)	119 – Synth Drum	60 – Hi Bongo
15 – Tubular Bells	50 – String Ensemble 2	85 – Lead 5 (charang)	120 – Reverse Cymbal	61 – Low Bongo
16 – Dulcimer	51 – SynthStrings 1	86 – Lead 6 (voice)	121 – Guitar Fret Noise	62 – Mute Hi Conga
17 – Drawbar Organ	52 – SynthStrings 2	87 – Lead 7 (fifths)	122 – Breath Noise	63 – Open Hi Conga
18 – Percussive Organ	53 – Choir Aahs	88 – Lead 8 (bass+lead)	123 – Seashore	64 – Low Conga
19 – Rock Organ	54 – Choir Oohs	89 – Pad 1 (new age)	124 – Bird Tweet	65 – High Timbale
20 – Church Organ	55 – Synth Voice	90 – Pad 2 (warm)	125 – Telephone Ring	66 – Low Timbale
21 – Reed Organ	56 – Orchestral Hit	91 – Pad 3 (polysynth)	126 – Helicopter	67 – High Agogo
22 – Accordion	57 – Trumpet	92 – Pad 4 (choir)	127 – Applause	68 – Low Agogo
23 – Harmonica	58 – Trombone	93 – Pad 5 (bowed)	128 – Gunshot	69 – Cabasa
24 – Tango Accordion	59 – Tuba	94 – Pad 6 (metallic)	35 – Acoustic Bass Drum	70 – Maracas
25 – Nylon Sting Guitar	60 – Muted Trumpet	95 – Pad 7 (halo)	36 – Bass Drum 1	71 – Short Whistle
26 – Steel String Guitar	61 – French Horn	96 – Pad 8 (sweep)	37 – Side Stick	72 – Long Whistle
27 – Electric Jazz Guitar	62 – Brass Section	97 – FX 1 (rain)	38 – Acoustic Snare	73 – Short Guiro
28 – Electric Clean Guitar	63 – SynthBrass 1	98 – FX 2 (soundtrack)	39 – Hand Clap	74 – Long Guiro
29 – Electric Muted Guitar	64 – SynthBrass 2	99 – FX 3 (crystal)	40 – Electric Snare	75 – Claves
30 – Overdxriven Guitar	65 – Soprano Sax	100 – FX 4 (atmosphere)	41 – Low Floor Tom	76 – Hi Wood Block
31 – Distortion Guitar	66 – Alto Sax	101 – FX 5 (brightness)	42 – Closed Hi-Hat	77 – Low Wood Block
32 – Guitar Harmonics	67 – Tenor Sax	102 – FX 6 (goblins)	43 – High Floor Tom	78 – Mute Cuica
33 – Acoustic Bass	68 – Baritone Sax	103 – FX 7 (echoes)	44 – Pedal Hi-Hat	79 – Open Cuica
34 – Electric Bass (finger)	69 – Oboe	104 – FX 8 (sci-fi)	45 – Low Tom	80 – Mute Triangle
35 – Electric Bass (pick)	70 – English Horn	105 – Sitar	46 – Open Hi-Hat	81 – Open Triangle

Appendix C – Programming Code Help Sheet

Climbing and Falling

3 Ways to Control Movement

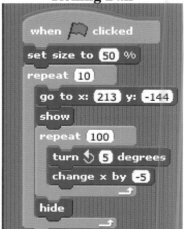

Bounce Off an Object

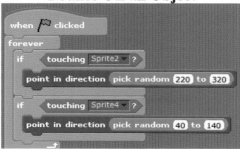

Jumping

Rolling Ball

Scrolling Background

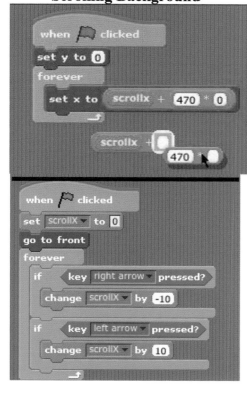

Shooting Something Out

Walk But Not Through

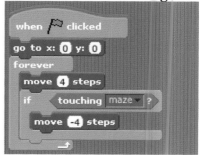

Move Across Screen

Appendix D – Going Further with Scratch (BYOB and Panther)

BYOB and Panther are two really good choices for allowing students to go further in programming with Scratch. They both offer advanced students an excellent opportunity to expand their programming skills. The downside is that because they were not developed by MIT, the files they create do not run in Scratch or upload to the Scratch website.

 **BYOB** (Build Your Own Blocks) is an extension to Scratch developed by Jens Mönig and Brian Harvey from the University of Cailfornia, Berkeley. (It is also known as Snap!.) It allows the user to create their own, customized programming blocks (thus the acronym) and enables the use of recursion (a more advanced programming concept). A more comprehensive description can be found at http://wiki.scratch.mit.edu/wiki/BYOB. It is available for free at http://byob.berkeley.edu. (BYOB projects have a .ypr suffix.)

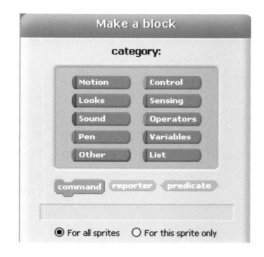

 **Panther** is another extension to Scratch. It was developed by a group of programmers (some very young) who felt that Scratch was lacking advanced features. Panther adds two new programming palettes – Files (for manipulating saved files) and Colors (allowing greater color creation and control). Panther also adds various programming blocks to the original palettes, including camera options, vertical / horizontal stretching, making blocks draggable, and cloning/deleting sprites. Another benefit is allowing the user to set the graphics quality (good – normal – fast) for improved performance. A good synopsis of all of the changes can be found at http://wiki.scratch.mit.edu/wiki/Panther. Panther is available for free at http://pantherprogramming.weebly.com. Currently, Panther does not seem to run on Macintosh, only Windows (though there is a work-around for Ubuntu). (Panther projects have a .pnt suffix.)

5994140R00032

Printed in Great Britain
by Amazon.co.uk, Ltd.,
Marston Gate.